Festiniog in Colour

Ffestiniog Mewn Lliw

Peter Johnson & Michael Whitehouse

IAN ALLAN
Publishing

First published 1995

ISBN 0 7110 2355 7

Published by Ian Allan Publishing an imprint of Ian Allan Ltd, Terminal House, Station Approach, Shepperton, Surrey TW17 8AS.

Printed by Ian Allan Printing Ltd, Coombelands House, Coombelands Lane, Addlestone, Weybridge, Surrey KT15 1HY.

Front cover:
On 19 September 1955 *Prince* passes Pen Cob. The loco is equipped with only the small whistle, the larger one probably having been stolen during the period of the line's closure. *Prince*'s Norwegian coupler replaced the previously-used chain-link coupling and probably came from a carriage. The carriages are No 23, formerly of the North Wales Narrow Gauge and the Welsh Highland Railways, and No 12, the first to be put back into service.
P. B. Whitehouse/
C. M. Whitehouse Collection

Back cover:
In April 1993 *Merddin Emrys* arrives at Minffordd with a Down train and much steam in evidence.
Peter Johnson

Introduction

As the Festiniog Railway staggered towards the middle years of the 20th century, becoming more and more decrepit, memories of its glorious past were still retained fondly, mainly by outsiders, enthusiasts and tourists. The decline of this pre-eminent narrow gauge railway has been said to have followed the death of Charles Easton Spooner in 1889, for none of his successors proved to have the Spooner family's flair for the line, in either directorial, managerial or engineering aspects. In practical terms, however, serious decline set in after a quar-rymen's strike in 1913, reducing the FR's revenue and, thus, the amount spent on routine maintenance. World War 1 aggra-vated the situation and the railway never recovered, closing to passengers in 1939 and completely in 1946.

The high regard for the FR held it in good stead, for it was not forgotten and neglected. Vigorous efforts by its admirers saw a team led by Alan Pegler, and supported by the Festiniog Railway Society, gaining control in 1954. The Festiniog revival had begun.

Forty years after Festiniog Railway passenger services recom-menced in 1955 it has regained its former pre-eminence, with many great achievements, the 27-year task of restoring the line to Blaenau Ffestiniog not least amongst them. Other achieve-ments vary in scope from the restoration of 19th century loco-motives and carriages to the construction of two double Fairlie locomotives and 16 bogie carriages at Boston Lodge, the automation of passing loops and the operation of a centrally-heated push-pull six-car diesel train.

Over the past 40 years the appearance of the Railway has changed considerably, too. From the stations to the carriage fleet, not forgetting, of course, the locomotives, the Railway has developed and improved. The locomotive fleet has been supplemented, both by acquisition and new build, converted from coal to oil-burning, though not without some degree of controversy when first brought in. The engines are now turned out in varied liveries, not all with a historical basis, providing

variety from the standard green introduced in 1955. The carriage fleet, likewise, has been augmented, and liveries range from green and cream, 'varnished mahogany', cherry red to the present red and off-white arrangement.

The trains themselves have progressed considerably since the 1950s, when, naturally, only original Festiniog stock was available. Nowadays trains often include wooden, aluminium, or steel-bodied carriages with corridor connections, toilet and buffet facilities, as well as older stock, including the oldest four-wheel and bogie carriages in regular use in the world.

The 19th century stock has recently been turned out in historical liveries, a vital attribute much appreciated by observers and photographers during vintage train operation. Since the first operation of such a train, in 1982, when the formation consisted of three four-wheelers and four bogie cars, great effort has been put into recreating authentic trains of the past, both in appearance and formation. Despite being a service for which no tickets are sold, gravity trains have proved unexpectedly popular with observers; developed from this has been mixed train operation, too. Interest in the vintage trains has culminated in the now annual vintage weekends, when attempts are made to ensure that all modern stock is confined to depot, although no-one has yet been heard to complain about the operation of 1992-built Fairlie *David Lloyd George* on such occasions!

During the big push to return Festiniog Railway operations to Blaenau Ffestiniog the appearance of both trains and line-side structures became sadly neglected. 1985 saw the start of an initiative to provide the Railway with some attractive gardens; the initiative developed to encompass structures, too. The effect can be seen, throughout the length of the line. Flower beds at Porthmadog, Minffordd and Penrhyn attract much favourable comment, as do the station buildings at Penrhyn, restored externally to 1880s appearance, internally a volunteers' hostel.

The Railway has not always aimed for authenticity in the provision of all its passenger facilities; indeed the most modern are provided at Porthmadog, Tan-y-bwlch and Blaenau Ffestiniog. Harbour station itself has been considerably extended to provide sales and catering facilities, as well as a museum and both terminal stations have recently acquired canopies. Other installations have also been adapted to meet modern requirements: the exchange yard at Minffordd now providing road/rail interchange as well as becoming the permanent way depot. The famous Boston Lodge Works have been extensively expanded and modernised, too.

The Festiniog Railway has come under the scrutiny of many thousands of photographers since the invention of photography, with the earliest known exposures being dated to the early 1870s. Since the restoration of the line commenced there can be very few trains which have escaped being recorded photographically. In the 1950s and 1960s most exposures would have been in monochrome due to the cost and low speed of colour transparency film; the speed of this material being the reason so many early colour photographs were only taken of static subjects on fine days, giving the impression that it never rained!

One of the small number of photographers using colour in the early years of the Festiniog's revival was the late Pat Whitehouse, some of whose photographs we are pleased to include here; he also collected some of the transparencies taken by other photographers and included here also. Pat Whitehouse came to be known as an author and as the founder of the Birmingham Railway Museum at Tyseley; he was in at the birth of railway preservation, the first secretary of the Talyllyn Railway Preservation Society before becoming involved with founding the Dart Valley Railway. In 1963 he wrote *Festiniog Railway Revival*, the first book to cover the Festiniog's rebirth, and published by the publisher of this present work, too. At the time of his death he was a patron of the Festiniog Railway Co.

The limitations of early colour photography, combined with the contemporary limitations of colour printing, mean that some of the older subjects illustrated here have rarely, if at all,

A trip up the line

The Festiniog Railway commenced life as a gravity railway, with horses pulling the empty wagons back up to the quarries. A press visit to publicise the railway's 1963 'Centenary of Steam' celebrations was arranged for 22 May that year, when horse power was demonstrated before an admiring crowd at Harbour station.
P. B. Whitehouse/ C. M. Whitehouse Collection

been seen in colour, and certainly not of the reproduction quality now available. (We still live in hope of finding someone who photographed the FR in colour before World War 2!)

We hope this small collection of photographs, with others of our own taken to bring the story up to date, will therefore show the revived Festiniog Railway's first 40 years in a new light. In the interests of quality it is not possible to present an exhaustive view of the railway's achievements but the collection does show how it has developed since it became one of the pioneers of the preservation movement.

Peter Johnson
Leicester
Michael Whitehouse
Worcester
November 1994

Note:
Although Blaenau Ffestiniog is the correct Welsh spelling for the railway's northern terminus, the Festiniog Railway was the name adopted by the Act of Parliament authorising the line. The book, therefore, uses 'Festiniog' when referring to the railway and 'Ffestiniog' when mentioning the town.

Title page:
The Festiniog Railway's oldest extant Fairlie, *Merddin Emrys* rolls around the Dduallt spiral as it returns its train to Porthmadog on 4 April 1993. Providing a contrast with the train's passengers, the tips of the Maenofferen Slate Quarry at Blaenau Ffestiniog in the distance indicate the source of so much of the railway's original traffic. *Peter Johnson*

During June 1993's Vintage Weekend *Palmerston*, then newly restored to working order, stands at Harbour station with replica Hudson toastrack No 39 and No 23, built for the North Wales Narrow Gauge Railway in 1894, obtained from the Welsh Highland Railway in 1936 and turned out in that line's livery following an overhaul completed earlier in 1993. Fairlie *David Lloyd George* arrives from Blaenau Ffestiniog with car No 10 adjacent to the loco.
Peter Johnson

Merddin Emrys sets off across the Cob, again during the 1993 Vintage Weekend. Next to the locomotive is quarrymen's coach No 8.
Peter Johnson

Opposite:
The Fairlie *Taliesin* with van No 1 and a slate wagon are pictured in Boston Lodge yard during September 1958. Despite the demolition of the foundry chimney in the 1970s and other changes the view is still recognisable today.
J. C. Flemons/C. M. Whitehouse Collection

Opposite:
Seen from the cliff top above Boston Lodge in the mid-1960s, *Prince* passes with a Down train. The area in the foreground, with car No 10 on the left, has seen extensive development over the intervening years; the carriage workshop and maintenance area are now where the rail was stacked, the frame structure, on the right, is now the locomotive shed and the long shed, for many years a loco shed, was demolished in the 1980s. On the right are the Peckett and *Welsh Pony*, partially protected from the elements. In the yard can be seen *Merddin Emrys* without its cab roof, *Moelwyn* and an England tender.
C. M. Whitehouse Collection

Left:
Prince takes water at the Toll Gate steps, Boston Lodge, on 19 September 1955. On the right are the gates, later removed, into the Top Yard.
P. B. Whitehouse/
C. M. Whitehouse Collection

Opposite:
Almost a traditional Festiniog
scene is recreated outside the
old Boston Lodge engine shed
on 5 September 1992 as
*Merddin Emrys, David Lloyd
George* and *Prince* pose for the
camera. At this stage *David
Lloyd George* was still incom-
plete, although operating, and
was painted black. *Peter
Johnson*

Left:
Approaching Lottie's Crossing
the now-complete *David Lloyd
George* is seen with the mass
of Moel-y-gest forming the
background during May 1994.
Peter Johnson

Right:
Prince leaves Minffordd in June 1957.

At this date the tracks are still grass-covered — an inheritance from the period of closure. Car No 11, next to *Prince*, would have observation-end windows installed during the following winter.

J. C. Flemons/C. M. Whitehouse Collection

Opposite:
On 14 July 1974 *Linda* heads for Dduallt. The train is photographed on Gwyndy Bank, one of the railway's famous dry-stone embankments.

C. M. Whitehouse

Left:
15 years on and the date is 19 August 1989. *Linda* is again the primary attraction as the locomotive heads a train on Gwyndy Bank. It is interesting to note the changes that have been made over the intervening period.
Peter Johnson

Below:
Blanche and train were photographed at Ty Fry on 16 April 1979. From the locomotives the carriages visible are Nos 15, 19, 116, 117 or 118, Buffet Car 103, 105 (with toilet) and Observation Car 100 or 101. A house has recently been built on this vantage point.
C. M. Whitehouse

Right:
Prince and a rake of vintage stock passes Ty Fry in August 1990. The Festiniog Railway is justly proud of its collection of historic coaching stock, and amongst the collection are the country's oldest bogie coaches. The Festiniog was the first railway, in the early 1870s, to operate bogie coaches on any line in Britain.
Peter Johnson

Opposite:
Approaching Penrhyn, *Merddin Emrys* is caught by the camera in May 1980. *Merddin Emrys*'s brass domes are now fitted to the 1979-built *Earl of Merioneth*.
Peter Johnson

Right:
David Lloyd George is pictured as it nears Rhiw Goch during May 1993. Semi-open tourist car No 38, next to the loco, was built at Boston Lodge in 1971, using the underframe of bogie wagon No 38. Ironically, the earlier No 38 was itself built on the underframe of a Hudson-built tourist car dating from the 1920s.
Peter Johnson

Opposite:
Merddin Emrys and most of the railway's available bogie stock are seen on Cei Mawr on 10 June 1965. This dry-stone embankment is 62ft high. Second from the rear is car No 14, the buffet car built from a Lynton & Barnstaple Railway vehicle in 1963. The green and ivory carriage livery was found to be too time-consuming for volunteers to apply and maintain so it was replaced by the short-lived 'varnished teak' and then by the long-lived cherry red. Spray-painting, introduced in the 1980s, allows more complicated liveries to be applied more quickly, to both carriages and locomotives.
Ken Cooper/C. M. Whitehouse Collection

Right:
As a result of tree growth views like this of *Prince* at Whistling Curve on 10 June 1965 are no longer possible. The unusual train formation, as the four-wheelers would normally be placed next to the locomotive, was due to the end vehicles only being fully fitted with vacuum brakes.
Ken Cooper/C. M. Whitehouse Collection

Opposite:
Also on 10 June 1965, a contrasting view at Whistling Curve sees *Linda* heading for Tan-y-bwlch. The 'varnished teak' carriage is No 104, the first of six wooden-bodied cars built at Boston Lodge between 1964 and 1970. These were known initially as 'Centenary' stock, arising from the 1965 centenary of passenger services, and then then later as 'Barns', because they had the same profile as No 14, the ex-Lynton & Barnstaple buffet car.
Ken Cooper/C. M. Whitehouse Collection

Opposite:
Blanche and *Linda* arrive at Tan-y-bwlch on 2 May 1993, during the gala held to celebrate the centenary of these locomotives. *Blanche* is carrying an original Hunslet oil-lamp and a birthday greetings gift tag.
Peter Johnson

Right:
Tan-y-bwlch became the restored railway's terminus in 1958. Attracting much attention, *Prince* waits to return to Portmadoc, possibly with a relief train, in the September of that year.
J. C. Flemons/C. M. Whitehouse Collection

Inset:
As a reminder of the Festiniog Railway's *raison d'être* demonstration gravity trains are now run quite often during special events. Here one is seen leaving Tan-y-bwlch for Minffordd during the June 1993 Vintage Weekend; the colour-light signal and the number of brakesmen are not prototypical!
Peter Johnson

Station mistress Bessie Jones and former East Coast main line driver (and well-known railway author) Bill Hoole, who retired to drive on the FR, pose with *Taliesin* in September 1958.
P. B. Whitehouse/ C. M. Whitehouse Collection

Evidence of the changes made at Tan-y-bwlch to cope with the large numbers who travelled there whilst it was a terminus are visible in this photograph taken on 5 April 1969. By this time the line had been extended to Dduallt; the 'old' *Earl of Merioneth* waits to return to Portmadoc; notice the attention given to the locomotive's bright-work, compared to older photographs.
C. M. Whitehouse

Right:
On 13 June 1993 *Palmerston*, with a special train for the Festiniog Railway Society's directors and guests, takes water from the new water tank at Tan-y-bwlch, all around much taken by the over-flow. *Peter Johnson*

Opposite:
A few minutes earlier than the scene in the previous photograph, *Earl of Merioneth* takes water at the original Tan-y-bwlch water tank. To cope with the demands of an increased service a second water tank had been mounted on a crib alongside the old one. *C. M. Whitehouse*

Opposite:
Fairlies cross at Tan-y-bwlch
on 4 April 1993 — *David Lloyd
George* was not named until
16 April of that year so when
this photograph was taken the
nameplates were still covered
up. On the left is the stone
base of the old water tank.
Peter Johnson

Left:
Mountaineer sets off across
Creuau Bank as it leaves Tan-
y-bwlch for Dduallt on 13 April
1971.
C. M. Whitehouse

Llyn Mair is an artificial lake and the Festiniog Railway runs around three sides of it. At Tafarn Trip *David Lloyd George* approaches the short Garnedd Tunnel with a mixed train in the rhododendron season on 20 June 1993.
Peter Johnson

Vintage diesel locomotive *Moelwyn* stands at Dduallt with a shuttle working with four-wheeled stock from Tan-y-bwlch on 4 August 1970, when the photographer was second man. Observe the various tools piled on the front of the loco.
C. M. Whitehouse

Opposite:
On 21 August 1972 *Merddin Emrys* is seen running round at Dduallt; the head-shunt was actually laid on the formation of the Deviation spiral, then under construction.
C. M. Whitehouse

Right:
The 'new' *Earl of Merioneth* is pictured at the rear of the Tanygrisiau pumped-storage power station, bound for Tanygrisiau, in May 1980; the CEGB's Penstocks are visible above the train.
Peter Johnson

Opposite:
Merddin Emrys heads along the Deviation line near Tanygrisiau in May 1980. The second carriage is No 119, a steel-bodied vehicle built at Boston Lodge on an ex-Isle of Man Railways underframe and new in traffic that year. The third vehicle is Buffet car No 14 and next to that is No 116, the experimental aluminium-bodied vehicle built by Edmund Crow of Cleator Moor, Cumbria, in 1972; it was rebuilt with new opening windows and doors in 1982.
Peter Johnson

Opposite:
With Llyn Ystradau and its dam behind, *David Lloyd George* climbs towards Porthmadog with a rake of push-pull stock in May 1993. The Festiniog's first experimental operation of push-pull services occurred 20 years ago, in 1975, when services were introduced over the completed section of the Dduallt Deviation. Regular operation of push-pull services with a full driving-trailer is, however, a product of the 1990s and the construction of purpose-built coaches.
Peter Johnson

Left:
With the Moelwyns behind, *Mountaineer* nears the Stwlan Dam road crossing with a morning train in late-August 1992. Car No 11 is apparently substituting for push-pull driving trailer No 111.
Peter Johnson

Right:
Mountaineer's profile is shown
to good effect as the locomotive leaves Tanygrisiau station
to rejoin the original line in the
autumn of 1988; the
photographer's vantage point is
now the site of Tanygrisiau's
signalbox.
Peter Johnson

Below right:
Linda leaves Blaenau
Ffestiniog in September 1983;
the BR line to Llandudno
Junction and Blaenau's disused
town hall are behind the train.
This section of railway, for
both gauges, was partly funded
by the local authorities and by
the EEC.
Peter Johnson

Opposite:
The present station at Blaenau
Ffestiniog was opened in two
stages, with the BR platform
being brought into use on
22 March 1982. On that date
Blanche 'just happened' to be
in use to deliver the FR's buffer
stops, arriving at the same time
as BR's inaugural train. Unlike
the occasion of the FR's
Blaenau reopening, on 25 May
1982, and when Tanygrisiau
reopened, on 24 June 1978, the
weather was fine.
Peter Johnson

THE LOCOMOTIVES
The Englands

Opposite:
Prince is the oldest of the Festiniog engines in service, being delivered as a side tank locomotive by George England & Co in 1864. A new boiler had been obtained for *Prince* during World War 2 so it became the first Festiniog locomotive to be restored, re-entering service in August 1955. It is seen waiting for passengers for the 11.30am departure on 19 September that year.
P. B. Whitehouse/
C. M. Whitehouse Collection

Left:
Work continued after the line's reopening to bring *Prince* up to fine fettle and the locomotive is seen running round at Tan-y-bwlch in 1958, with its tender still in undercoat.
P. B. Whitehouse/
C. M. Whitehouse Collection

Right:
A classic view of *Prince* at Boston Lodge on 13 September 1963; when this green paint was stripped off during *Prince*'s overhaul during the 1970s evidence was found of its Victorian livery and lining. *Ken Cooper/C. M. Whitehouse Collection*

Below right:
Prince was withdrawn for overhaul in 1968. However, the task was not started until 1974 and was only completed in 1980. During the overhaul the locomotive had its boiler superheated and was converted to oil-firing. The celebration of the Festiniog's 'Steam 125' in 1988 was to see *Prince*'s Victorian livery restored, setting a precedent for historic, and other, liveries for other members of the loco-motive fleet, and one which was to spread to the carriage fleet, too. The photograph was taken during the Festiniog Railway Society's 40th anniver-sary celebrations on 25 September 1994; the loco was about to work a 'Vintage Shuttle' to Minffordd. The fourth vehicle from the loco-motive is car No 7, the 'flying bench'; this is an early observa-tion car which now sees occasional use after many years on museum display. *Peter Johnson*

Like *Prince*, *Palmerston* is an England-built locomotive, although for many years it was considered an unrestorable wreck. In 1974 the locomotive was sold for restoration and moved to England. It eventually returned to Boston Lodge, where restoration was completed by a volunteer team in 1993. Unlike *Prince* no attempt has been made to modify the locomotive to suit current operating conditions so, apart from a new boiler, it remains little changed from its 19th century condition. *Palmerston* also remains coal-fired and, as a result, its use is limited. In June 1994 it returns to Porthmadog with vintage stock.
Peter Johnson

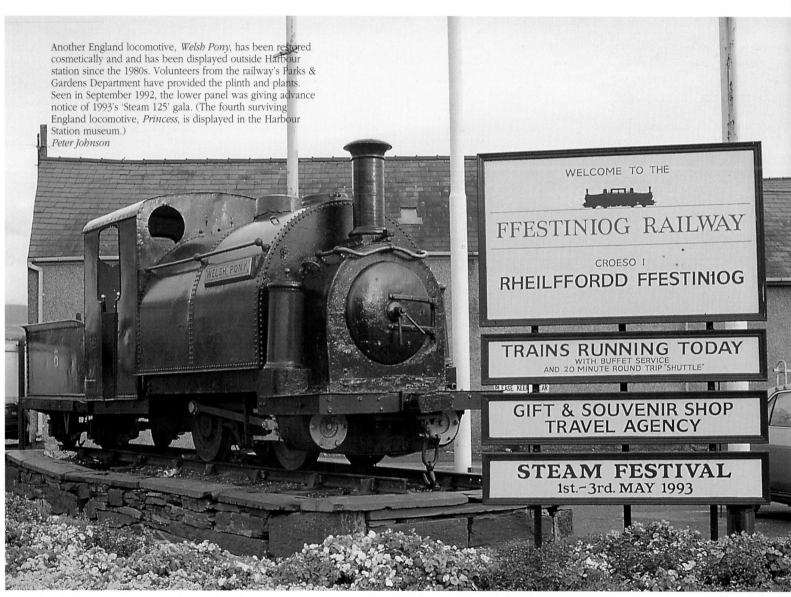

Another England locomotive, *Welsh Pony*, has been restored cosmetically and and has been displayed outside Harbour station since the 1980s. Volunteers from the railway's Parks & Gardens Department have provided the plinth and plants. Seen in September 1992, the lower panel was giving advance notice of 1993's 'Steam 125' gala. (The fourth surviving England locomotive, *Princess*, is displayed in the Harbour Station museum.)
Peter Johnson

WELCOME TO THE

FFESTINIOG RAILWAY

CROESO I
RHEILFFORDD FFESTINIOG

TRAINS RUNNING TODAY
WITH BUFFET SERVICE
AND 20 MINUTE ROUND TRIP "SHUTTLE"

GIFT & SOUVENIR SHOP
TRAVEL AGENCY

STEAM FESTIVAL
1st - 3rd. MAY 1993

The Fairlies

Above:
Built as *Livingston Thompson*
in 1886, *Taliesin* was the
second Fairlie built at Boston
Lodge; it was put back into
service in 1956 and is seen
running round at Harbour
station in 1958.
P. B. Whitehouse/
C. M. Whitehouse Collection

Left:
Taliesin was renamed *Earl of
Merioneth* in 1961, thereby
adopting one of HRH the Duke
of Edinburgh's titles. It is seen
with 'varnished teak' liveried
stock on 5 April 1969; this
carriage livery did not last very
long as it was found to wear at
different rates, making each
vehicle a different colour from
its neighbour. Evidence of
recent trackwork is visible in
the foreground.
C. M. Whitehouse

Left:

Left:
Almost at the end of its working career, the 'old' *Earl of Merioneth* is pictured with freshly-painted cherry-red liveried stock on 4 August 1970. The locomotive was withdrawn in 1971 and in 1988 was restored cosmetically as *Livingston Thompson* and loaned for display at the National Railway Museum, York. Van No 1, next to the loco, was built by the FR Society's Midland Group as a homework project in 1964, using some ironwork from a quarrymen's coach; from 1987 it has been allocated to the Civil Engineering Dept.
C. M. Whitehouse

Below:
Merddin Emrys was the first double Fairlie built at Boston Lodge, in 1879, and was also the last in use before the FR closed in 1946. It was abandoned with water in its tanks and wet coal slack in its bunkers, consequently requiring extensive work carrying out, including provision of new welded tanks, before it could re-enter traffic. In 1961 it ran unfinished, with the tanks painted in red lead primer, as seen on 27 August that year.
Ken Cooper/C. M. Whitehouse Collection

Merddin Emrys is caught at the coaling stage on 12 April 1971. The locomotive was then running with a new Hunslet parallel boiler installed the previous year. The following year it was converted to oil-firing, the railway's answer to increasing claims for woodland fires; the entire main line fleet was converted between 1971 and 1980. *Merddin Emrys* also ran for several years without dome covers, as seen here. Shovelling coal on the right is Evan Davies, now the FR's senior driver and longest-serving employee.
C. M. Whitehouse

Left:
In 1986/87 *Merddin Emrys* underwent a major overhaul when as much as possible of its pre-1946 style was restored and its late 1880s livery was applied. On a fine afternoon in August 1991 *Merddin Emrys* is pictured about to go on shed.
Peter Johnson

Right:
The 'new' *Earl of Merioneth* entered service in 1979, using a new Hunslet parallel boiler and the bogies and some other components from the 'old' *Earl*. It is seen leaving Tan-y-bwlch carrying a headboard recording the achievement of the first Fairlie built since 1911; the occasion was the Festiniog Railway Society's 25th anniversary in September 1979.
Peter Johnson

Opposite:
In 1989 attempts were made to soften the 'new' *Earl of Merioneth*'s rather harsh lines, by fitting the chimneys and brass domes previously on *Merddin Emrys* and adopting a new paint-scheme. In this condition *Earl of Merioneth* is seen passing Pen Cob in August 1991.
Peter Johnson

Right:
When it came to building *David Lloyd George* in 1992 every attempt was made to preserve the traditional Fairlie appearance, even down to installing a taper boiler. It is seen at Porthmadog with *Merddin Emrys* on 2 May 1993.
Peter Johnson

Acquired Locomotives

Opposite:
The Hunslet Engine Co of Leeds built *Linda* and *Blanche* for Lord Penrhyn in 1893. *Linda* came to the Festiniog on loan in 1962, being purchased the following year. For FR use it was given one of the spare England tenders. In 1969 its boiler was superheated and in 1970 it became a 2-4-0STT. In the winter of 1970/71 it became the first loco to be converted to oil-firing and is seen in that condition, being prepared for duty at Boston Lodge on 11 April 1971.
C. M. Whitehouse

PORTMADOC

On 21 August 1985 *Linda* is seen as reconverted to a coal-burner, this time as a gas producer. The conversion work carried out included considerable modifications to the locomotive's front-end draughting arrangements and the fitting of a Lempor-type chimney. The project was considered a success, with much higher superheat temperatures being obtained; a self-cleaning spark arrestor prevented problems in woodland, too. In 1986 *Linda* was converted back to oil-firing following a reduction in the price of gas oil, the draughting modifications remaining in place subsequently.
Peter Johnson

In 1991 *Linda*'s tender was modified by the addition of a removable aluminium cab section, the loco being turned out in a white-lined midnight-blue livery at the same time. In September 1994 the original Hunslet chimney was restored, all changes being visible in this photograph, taken of a Down train passing the restored Toll Gate on 16 October 1994.
Peter Johnson

Opposite:
In the early days of oil-firing problems were found with the higher temperatures generated burning the smokebox paint; until a heat-resistant black paint could be found aluminium was used, amidst not a little controversy. *Linda* is seen thus on 3 April 1972.
C. M. Whitehouse

Opposite:
Blanche was obtained from the Penrhyn Quarry Railway in 1963. Two years later the locomotive received a new tender with half-cab. With the paintwork still in good condition it is seen on 10 April 1966.
Ken Cooper/C. M. Whitehouse Collection

Left:
In 1972 *Blanche* was rebuilt as a 2-4-0STT with new piston-valve cylinders and superheating; it was converted to oil-firing at the same time. The photograph was taken, following completion of a major overhaul, on 27 August 1994.
Peter Johnson

Opposite:
Linda and *Blanche* have proved to be both successful and reliable on the Festiniog. In 1993 a major event was held to commemorate their centenary; one of the attractions was the loan of several visiting quarry Hunslets. These included 'elder brother' *Charles* (built by Hunslet in 1882), which was loaned as a static exhibit from the National Trust at Penrhyn Castle. The three locomotives are seen at Boston Lodge on 3 May 1993.
Peter Johnson

Left:
Built for War Department Light Railways use in 1917, *Mountaineer* was a product of the American Loco Co of Paterson, New Jersey. From 1935 it was used on the Tramway de Pithiviers à Toury until that line, a roadside tramway, closed in 1964. It was bought by John Ransom, then a Festiniog Railway Society director, and in 1967 brought to the FR. It was modified to fit the FR's restricted loading gauge and put to work, being photographed with the 10.20am for Dduallt on 3 September 1969. The bell came from the original *Mountaineer* but it was removed after a while as the crews found its noise to be unnerving.
E. D. Bruton/Festiniog Railway Magazine Collection

Mountaineer, photographed in October 1988, was converted to burn oil in 1971, when its smokebox and chimney were at first painted aluminium, and received a new all-welded superheated boiler and piston valves in 1982; the Fairlie-outline cab was fitted in 1983. The nameplates were cast from the surviving patterns made for the England-built *Mountaineer*. *Peter Johnson*

Internal Combustion Locomotives

The first loco to see action on the revived Festiniog was the armoured Simplex, later named *Mary Ann*, built in 1917 for the War Department and acquired by the FR in 1923. In 1994 it was put back into working order, after a period out of use, with original features restored and a military livery applied. Photographed on 25 September 1994 whilst Van No 2 was being turned on a wagon turntable at Boston Lodge. *Peter Johnson*

Right:
Moelwyn is a diesel locomotive obtained by the Festiniog Railway for shunting duties in 1925. It had been built by Baldwin with a 45hp petrol engine for the French Government Artillery Railways in 1918. In 1956 it was over-hauled and a Gardner diesel engine installed, with the loco-motive being available for service from August that year. The following year it was converted from a 0-4-0DM to a 2-4-0DM to improve the ride. A vacuum brake was fitted in 1966 and in that form it was photographed shunting at Porthmadog on 15 April 1968.
C. M. Whitehouse

Inset:
Built for the Royal Navy's 2ft 6in gauge Chattenden & Upnor Railway, by Hibberd in 1954, *Upnor Castle* was first obtained by the Welshpool & Llanfair Light Railway in 1962 before coming to the Festiniog Railway in 1968. It entered service, after modifications, in August that year. The main FR passenger diesel until Conway Castle became available in 1986, it was re-engined in 1971 and 1980. It is seen arriving at Penrhyn with the 9.40am service from Porthmadog on 21 August 1972. It is clearly a hot day as the locomotive's side sheets are raised to improve ventilation! From the rear of the train the carriages are Nos 11, 12, 20, 17 and 18, all of which date from between 1876 and 1880.
C. M. Whitehouse

Another Hibberd, albeit built in 1958, *Conway Castle* came to the Festiniog Railway from the Royal Naval Armaments Depot at Ernesettle, near Plymouth. Arriving in Wales in 1982 it was regauged from 2ft 6in, fitted for push-pull working and given a new superstructure before entering service in 1986. It is shown passing the rear of Capel Nazareth (left) in Penrhyndeudraeth with an early morning staff special on 30 April 1994. The push-pull facility made termination of the service at Penrhyn an easy matter.
Peter Johnson

Privately owned and visiting locos

Right:
Hunslet built *Britomart* for the Pen-yr-orsedd Quarry in 1899. In 1963 it was purchased by a group of Festiniog staff and volunteers who transferred it to Boston Lodge and got it working in 1966. Remaining coal-fired it has since been used on owners' specials and has made appearances at FR events. It is seen at Boston Lodge on 30 October 1966.
Ken Cooper/C. M. Whitehouse Collection

Opposite:
Sgt. Murphy was built by Kerr, Stewart of Stoke-on-Trent in 1918 and was first used by the Navy. In 1920 it went to the Penrhyn Slate Quarries and remained there until sold for preservation in 1964. From 1977 until 1991 it was displayed at the Conwy Valley Railway Museum at Betws-y-Coed. Two changes of ownership that year saw it acquired by the Festiniog Railway's general manager who had it restored at the Penrhyndeudraeth works of Winson Engineering. It is seen passing Ty Fry on 4 April 1993, shortly after restoration was complete and before the loco had been lined out.
Peter Johnson

Left:
Alice was built by Hunslet for the Dinorwic Slate Quarries at Llanberis in 1902. Restoration, including fitting a new boiler, started at the Bala Lake Railway in the 1980s and was completed at Boston Lodge in 1994. It is seen there, undergoing a steam test, on 24 August 1993. *Alice* is now located on the Leighton Buzzard Railway in Bedfordshire. To the right behind *Alice* is the Boston Lodge yard shunter, also Hunslet-built, *Harold*. This 39hp diesel was built in 1979 and was given to the FR by Yorkshire Water in 1993; North Brierley sewage works had been its previous location.
Peter Johnson

Below:
The 1993 event to commemorate the centenaries of *Linda* and *Blanche* has already been mentioned. *Charles* is seen at Boston Lodge with the summit of Snowdon visible through the cab. The recently restored gunpowder wagon is an example of one of the few private-owner wagons to have run on the Festiniog; unusually, the slate wagons, although allocated to specific quarries, were owned by the railway company.
Peter Johnson

Opposite:
Lilla was supplied new to the Cilgwyn Quarry in 1897, passing to the Penrhyn Quarries in 1928. After six years out of use it was bought by Bernard Latham in 1963 and arrived at the FR for the *Linda/Blanche* centenary gala after a brief stay at the Bala Lake Railway. *Lilla* stayed at the FR after the gala and was used occasionally on works trains and on non-public passenger trains. In addition, on one occasion, it also hauled a photographers' freight charter. On 4 May 1993 waggons were being shunted at Harbour station. It is now withdrawn for boiler inspection and overhaul.
Peter Johnson

Left:
Una came to the *Linda/Blanche* centenary gala on loan from the Welsh Slate Centre at Llanberis — the former Dinorwic workshops which have been its home since 1977. The locomotive was built by Hunslet in 1905 and, like *Britomart*, was supplied new to the Pen-yr-orsedd Slate Quarry in the Nantlle Vale. It is seen shunting skips at the rear of the Boston Lodge carriage workshops on 2 May 1993.
Peter Johnson

Five Festiniog locomotives were lined-up at Harbour station on 5 September 1992.
From the left they are *Prince, David Lloyd George, Merddin Emrys* (in steam),
Mountaineer (in steam) and *Linda*, just leaving with the 9.45am departure.
Peter Johnson